RAINBIRD
The Tragedy of an Artist

A Stage Play
Peter Mortimer

First published 2018 by IRON Press
5 Marden Terrace
Cullercoats
North Shields
NE30 4PD
tel +44(0)191 2531901
ironpress@xlnmail.com
www.ironpress.co.uk

ISBN 978-1-9997636-1-9
Printed by imprintdigital.com

© Peter Mortimer 2018

Cover and book Design Brian Grogan
Cover photo; Rainbird painting
All Quiet on the Western Front

Typeset in Georgia

IRON Press books are distributed by NBN International
and represented by Inpress Ltd
Churchill House, 12 Mosley Street,
Newcastle upon Tyne, NE1 1DE
tel: +44(0)191 2308104
www.inpressbooks.co.uk

RAINBIRD

HOW IT CAME ABOUT

Victor Noble Rainbird lived a relatively short, eventful if often tragic life. Born in Sidney Street North Shields in December 1887, he died in March 1936, aged only 47 and was buried in a pauper's grave for 80 years.

Few can dispute that he was a talented painter. And prolific. Though he painted throughout his life, creating a vast volume of work, most of his best paintings were probably pre-World War One.

He was the only northern artist to be accepted by the Royal Academy in London in 1911 and his painting career was in full flow when war was declared in 1914. Rainbird had been given various awards and prizes and the British Army recognised his talents, choosing him to sketch the enemy positions from the hazardous territory of No Man's Land, an 'honour' which may well have contributed to his decline.

Shell shock and gas poisoning took their effect. Cancer eventually took hold, his marriage fell apart and he turned to alcohol often knocking out quick sketches or paintings in the pubs of North Shields to pay for his liquor.

My own interest in the artist stemmed from seeing an exhibition of his work at The Low Light, North Shields in 2015. This exhibition was put together by David Young who also gave a fascinating talk on the painter - I was hooked.

It's fair to say that without David Young this play could never have been written. He provided me with a detailed timeline of Rainbird's life, fed me a whole welter of other information and also managed to raise £6,500 to create a beautiful headstone (sculpted by the artist Neil Talbot) to enhance the pauper's grave. This was unveiled on March 8, 2016 in a special (and very crowded) memorial and unveiling service at Christ Church and Preston Cemetery.

Rainbird dwelt within me for three years as I grappled to make dramatic sense of him. By 2016, despite my early fumbling attempts I had little idea how I would tackle the play but, with the blind confidence (mixed with a terrifying panic) of the playwright, myself and *Cloud Nine Theatre Company* set about raising the £25,000 funding which would make a full-scale professional production possible here in Rainbird's own town. We succeeded. I enrolled in Clare Money's art classes on the Shields Fish Quay, the better to understand the mind of a painter.

Clare was wonderfully patient and supportive and nurtured me to create several *jejune* paintings of my own, including a portrait of Rainbird himself and one of my partner, the writer Kitty Fitzgerald.

I visited the Royal Academy, whose lecture rooms are little changed from Rainbird's day. I talked to painter friends. I decided the play would have two threads, one in Rainbird's time, one modern-day.

We had a successful art auction at the Exchange to raise more funds. This was great fun and brought in £2,200.

Though I'm mainly a contemporary playwright, four of my own plays have been historical. You learn to respect history and respect your subject matter, but never be enslaved by it. You base things on fact but make up a great deal – you have to. It is the spirit of the play that counts. It is the essence the writer seeks to capture, not every tiny detail. You do tons of research and use maybe one per cent of it.

I'm thrilled we're presenting the play at The Exchange which under the tireless work of Karen Knox and team has revived this previously moribund venue, so that now it is well on the way to becoming a vibrant theatre, gallery, restaurant and bar in a town that has long been starved of such a vital resource. *Cloud Nine* now sees The Exchange as their home.

We have also employed the talents of two artists; Josh Mayne to paint the 'self-portrait' of Rainbird vital for the play and Jan Brown who has organised art students at Tyne Coast College, Queen Alexandra site to do portraits of actors Jamie Brown and Heather Carroll. These will be displayed at The Exchange prior to the production. Clare also worked with Pearl Saddington doing workshops in Sunderland schools. The play is directed by that stalwart of North East theatre, writer, director and actor Neil Armstrong, with a whole string of successful *Cloud Nine* productions under his belt. 2018 is the company's 20th anniversary so a little hurrah there for the survival.

Late on, I came across a poem about Rainbird by the contemporary Cullercoats poet, Harry Gallagher. I liked this enough to include it in the book. A small detail to end. You may notice that one of our two support actors is none other than Dave Young, my inspiration for writing the play. This seems fitting somehow.

Peter Mortimer – April 2018

The Portrait Workshops

As part of the *Rainbird* project twenty Fine Art students from the Queen Alexandra site of Tyne Coast College, took part in sessions painting the two actors, Jamie Brown and Heather Carroll who play Victor and Liz Rainbird in the play. Their paintings were exhibited during the play's run at the Exchange, North Shields.

Photos by Jan Brown

DIRECTOR'S NOTES

I've directed shows on and off for Cloud Nine for about twenty years now. A lot of them have been plays written by Pete. These plays have forced me to get my head around numerous theatrical challenges involving a cast size of anything from a one man show to a cast of twenty. There have been tales of comic absurdity – *The Stolen Rubber Band,* or *A Parcel for Mr. Smith,* or *She's on Toast*; naturalistic pieces such as *Clockman*, social dramas such as *Chain* and historical plays like *Death at Dawn* (originally directed by Jackie Fielding). I've also tackled dozens of sketches, mimed pieces and the odd song along the way all of which have had their own little quirks and considerations to contend with. We have performed them in venues as diverse as a Yoga Station, countless pubs, village halls, theatres and on one occasion platform one of Whitley Bay Metro Station.

So we come to *Rainbird*. When Pete first asked me to direct this piece I must be honest, I'd never heard of the artist, but now I have and I'm pleased I have. I love his paintings and anything we can do to help preserve the memory of this remarkable man and his art is, I think, worth the effort. To achieve what he did from such humble North East beginnings really is quite remarkable – especially in those days. I should imagine a lad from Tyneside telling everyone he was off to paint the world was met with more than one raised eyebrow. I myself grew up in the 1970s in Seaham Harbour and was met with similar raised eyebrows when I annnounced I was off for a life in the theatre. So I hope I've been able to empathise a little with this man's struggle in order to re-create the story of his life here in his home town of North Shields.

Neil Armstrong

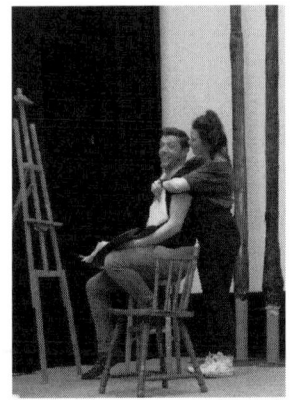

  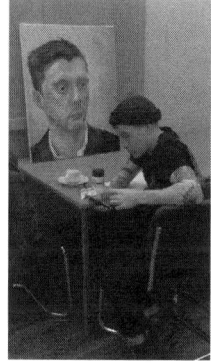

The photos show the cast's initial read-through plus early rehearsals. Top right (above) is the artist Joshua Mayne with his completed Rainbird 'self portrait'.

Photos by Kirstie Mackin and Dave Turnbull

WHO THEY ARE

JACOB ANDERTON (*Clive*) Graduated from Northumbria University in 2012 with a degree in Drama and Scriptwriting. His theatre credits include everything from pantomimes to playing Hamlet in theatre space North East's open air production. Most recently he performed in Alphabetti's touring production *The Frights* as Kieron. In more recent times Jacob has began to work more often in film and TV. His credits include Isaac Hedley in ITV's *Dark Angel*, private black in the *The War Inside* and Dodge in *Ripper*. Jacob is chuffed to be back in theatre especially in the North East.

NEIL ARMSTRONG (*Director*) was born in Seaham Harbour and began his theatrical career with The Red and White Theatre Company. His writing has been nominated by BAFTA, The National Comedy Awards and The Writers Guild of great Britain. He has directed for The Gala Theatre Durham, The Customs House, Arts Centre Washington and a host of independent companies. Neil has appeared in dozens of TV dramas, theatre plays and has been the resident panto villain at The Gala Theatre for the last ten years. He is working on a series of thrillers for The National Trust, *Tales from the Room* and his play about Grace Darling *Painting Grace* will tour in Autumn 2018.

SARAH BOULTER (*Hayley*) is a North-East actor who has performed in a number of shows in the region. She has recently played various roles in *Bankers* at Alphabetti Theatre, as well as touring the country with Northumberland Theatre Company's adaptation of Charles Dickens' *Barnaby Rudge*. She is delighted to be working with Cloud Nine Theatre Company and to be part of such a wonderful team. Other credits include; *Jack and The Beanstalk* (Gala Theatre, Durham) *The Dolly Mixtures* (Customs House), Catherine Cookson's *The Cinder Path*, *Waiting For Gateaux* (Ion Productions) *The Miscast Bard, Shakers* (Less is More Theatre Company), *Capital Schmities* (Live Theatre).

JAMIE BROWN (*Rainbird*) is a Gateshead lad, who trained at Bretton Hall and has worked extensively across the UK since 2006. Highlights include originating the roles of Harry Clasper (*Hadaway Harry* - Theatre Royal, London, NE tour) and John Simpson Kirkpatrick (*The Man and The Donkey* - Customs House) for which roles, he was named Performing Artist of the Year at the Journal Culture Awards in 2016. He also featured as Pvt. Henry Stevens in *Cloud Nine's* premiere production of *Death at Dawn* as well as its subsequent North-East tour. Elsewhere, he has done stints with Warner Brothers, BBC, and the Royal Opera House amongst many others.

HEATHER CARROLL (*Liz*) is excited to be once again working with *Cloud Nine Theatre*. She graduated from ALRA North with an MA in Professional Acting, is co-founder of troublehouse theatre and an Associate Artist with Actors for Human Rights. Credits include: Rosie in *The Terminal Velocity of Snowflakes* (Live Theatre), Susan in *Remains* (troublehouse theatre/Bolton Octagon). Tigerlily in *Daydream Believers* (Tmesis Theatre), Lex in *Raw* (troublehouse theatre) for which Heather was nominated for a Manchester Theatre Award, Best Performance Claudette/Bella in *Death at Dawn* (Cloud Nine) for which Heather won a Journal Culture Award for Best Newcomer.

MICHAEL CARRUTHERS (*Fust, Magistrate, Augustus John*) trained at Rose Bruford College. For over 30 years he has been a jobbing actor, doing everything from pantomime to Shakespeare. Based in North East England he has worked with many local companies including Northern Stage, 1399 Theatre Company and was a founder member of Three Over Eden. In recent years he has been involved with the performance team at Alnwick Castle in Northumberland. Michael is also a writer and has several screenplays and TV scripts in development with Newcastle-based production company Scattered Pictures.

DALE JEWITT (*Functionary, Brockhurst, Barman*) studied drama at Northumbria University. He was accepted onto Northern Stage's artist development programme, in 2016, where he co-founded the company *Theatre Hoodang*. Professional credits include, Puddles in *Puddles' Big Adventure* (The Customs House), Prince David in *Snow White* (Mendes Management), Edwin in *The Dirty Flea Bitten Scrounging Bastard* (Cloud Nine), Merlin in *And the Cow Jumped into the Woods* (The Customs House), Don John/Dogberry in *Much Ado About Nothing* (Theatre Space North East), Robin Hood in *Robin Hood* (Theatre Space North East) and Prince Hal in *Henry IV Part I* (Theatre Space North East).

SEAN KENNY (*RA Clerk, Gallery Mgr, Farrington*) announced, rather dramatically, at the tender age of fourteen that he was going to be an actor. For better or worse he has remained true to that pledge and has been lucky enough to have continued to work for the past 29 years. *Rainbird* marks the fourth time Sean has collaborated with *Cloud Nine*. Film/tv credits include: *Byker Grove, George Gently, Vera, James Bond: Tomorrow Never Dies* and his personal favourite, *Star Wars: The Phantom Menace*. Stage credits include: Frank in *Educating Rita,* Polonius in *Hamlet,* Mercutio in *Romeo and Juliet*. Sean can also be found dressed as a wizard teaching broomstick lessons at Alnwick Castle.

LAWRENCE NEALE (*William, Sergeant*) is a graduate of performance at Northumbria University, Lawrence also has many years experience as a musician and street performer, singing with his Barbershop Quartet, Tyne Signature and performing with World Beaters Music and their internationally acclaimed show *Spark!* He is also a founding member of puppet theatre company 4M Puppets. Lawrence's theatre and televison credits include: *The Pitmen Painters* (BKL*) Heaven Eyes* (TSF*) Beyond the End of the Road* (November Club) *Vera* (ITV*) Inspector George Gently ,The Dumping Ground* (BBC) and *The Dirty Scrounging Flea Bitten Bastard* (Cloud Nine).

KYLE MORLEY (*Kenneth Rainbird, trainee clerk, soldier, council official*) is currently finishing his extended diploma in acting, aged 20 from North Shields, Kyle continues to pursue a career in the Performing Arts industry. He has previously worked with the National Youth Film Academy and supported Peter Mortimer's play, *Croak the King and a Change in the Weather*, in a bill coupled with a play by Kitty Fitzgerald, *Making Plans for Jessica*. Kyle says, 'I am thrilled to be involved in this fantastic piece of theatre. It's been amazing to work with everyone and I will continue to support the future of this show.'

PETER MORTIMER *(author)* founded *Cloud Nine* in 1998 for reasons that were unclear and simply kept going. He has published books of poetry, travel books with an unusual bent, a novella, books for children and written far too many plays for his own good. He penned weekly newspaper columns for various periodicals most of whom ended up sacking him. He also founded IRON Press before many people were born (1973) and IRON continues to bring out intriguing publications. For seven years, before newsprint (and he himself) was an endangered species, he was the North East drama critic for *The Guardian*.

DAVE YOUNG (*Ralph Liddle, College Head*) is from North Shields and tremendously proud of his home town. He is both a volunteer and trustee at the Low Light Heritage Centre on the North Shields Quay, where he has curated a number of their successful summer exhibitions including one in 2015 based upon the life of artist Victor Noble Rainbird. Dave's acting experience is limited to his involvement with a number of short comedy sketches directed by Peter Mortimer of *Cloud Nine*, and he looks forward to working (but mostly listening and learning) on this exciting production.

Rainbird

Rainbird's on the street again,
drunker than the night.
Brushless, potless, forgotten –
something about a life
left buried in the mud,
exploded dreams and blood.

Rainbird's on the street again,
late of the fusiliers.
Says he once had a future
that fell down about his ears.
He's wheezing, fitting, falling,
smells of something appalling.

Rainbird's on the street again,
can he paint us for a drink?
He sold his oils this morning
so perhaps a pint and some ink
for a portrait stark and grim
of a much beloved country
and what it did to him.

Harry Gallagher

RAINBIRD
The Tragedy of an Artist
Peter Mortimer

CAST
MODERN DAY

Sarah Boulter	Hayley
Jacob Anderton	Clive

THE PAST

Jamie Brown	Victor Noble Rainbird
Heather Carroll	Liz Rainbird, née Kirkley
Lawrence Neal	William Rainbird, army sergeant
Dale Jewitt	Functionary, Gerald Brockhurst (artist) North Shields barman
Michael Carruthers	Fust, Augustus John, army doctor, magistrate
Sean Kenney	Royal Academy clerk, army Major art gallery manager, Stephen Farrington
Dave Young	Ralph Liddle, college head
Kyle Morley	Jones (trainee clerk), soldier on western front Tynemouth council official

Other parts are played by members of the company. Some script changes may take place in rehearsal after the book has gone to print.

TECHNICAL

Neil Armstrong	Director
Emily Baxendale	Costume/Props
Alison Ashton	Set design/construction
Duncan Allan	Stage Manager
Kitty Fitzgerald	Producer
Jan Brown	Student workshops artist
Joshua Mayne	Rainbird 'self-portrait' artist
Brian Grogan	Publicity design
Kirstie Mackin, Dave Turnbull	Photography

The play takes place in the first half of the 20th century and the modern-day; it is set in the North East, the Royal Academy, London and on the Western Front.
With thanks to Alan Fidler for WW1 knowledge, Riverdale Hall Hotel, Bellingham for writing space, The Exchange for great patience. YourPrint department, Thompson Art for picture framing. Rainbird opened for seven performances on Mon April 23rd 2018 at the Exchange, North Shields.

    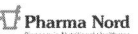

(MUSIC – WATER OF TYNE. FROM ONE SIDE OF THE STAGE ENTER HAYLEY. FROM THE OTHER SIDE. ENTER RAINBIRD. THEY PERFORM A DANCE OF SOME SORT TO SUGGEST A STRONG CONNECTION BETWEEN THEM.
AT THE END OF THE DANCE RAINBIRD EXITS. HAYLEY IS LEFT ALONE WHILE THE PRESENT-DAY SCENE EVOLVES AROUND HER. ENTER CLIVE. THEY ARE IN A SECOND HAND SHOP)

CLIVE Everything in this shop is junk, Second-hand junk at that. What is it exactly that attracts you to such places, Hayley?

HAYLEY Some of us like junk, Clive

CLIVE Junk here, junk there

HAYLEY *'Everywhere a junk-junk. Eeh aye, eeh aye o!'*

CLIVE Steady on. You'll get us thrown out

HAYLEY I know. You can't take me anywhere, can you? Look Clive, if you really don't like it in here, I'll meet you for a coffee in Fenwicks in 30 minutes. Leave your wife to do a bit of rummaging

CLIVE You might get off with that shop assistant. Some women go for 90 year old men

HAYLEY He's not a day over 85. Anyway, I just spotted some paintings over there

CLIVE Paintings?

HAYLEY You remember paintings, Clive? They're what I used to make when we were students

CLIVE A long time ago now

HAYLEY I suppose so. They say you never lose it though. Let's see (LOOKS AT PAINTINGS). Oh dear, not many Francis Bacons in here

CLIVE   Whoever he may be

HAYLEY   Stop trying to wind me up

CLIVE   I wasn't, actually (BEAT)

HAYLEY   (CARRIES ON) Sunsets….. pastoral splendour…… sweet little kittens..and – oh, that's unusual. That's very unusual

CLIVE   Found a Frankie Bacon, have you?

HAYLEY   There's the signature. Victor Noble Rainbird. But it's a self-portrait

CLIVE   Is that bad?

HAYLEY   As far as I know, Rainbird never painted a self-portrait

CLIVE   Well, obviously, he did. Whoever he is

HAYLEY   A North Shields artist. A good one

CLIVE   They have artists in North Shields?

HAYLEY   We should visit the fish quay together Clive. It's a fascinating place

CLIVE   I don't have to visit it. I can smell it from Tynemouth

HAYLEY   Very funny. Anyway, I read that Rainbird's paintings are just starting to come into fashion. But I've never heard of a Rainbird self-portrait

CLIVE   You mean it could be worth a bit of dosh?

HAYLEY   Yes, maybe

CLIVE   What, a few hundred, a thousand?

HAYLEY   Could be

CLIVE   Maybe more?

HAYLEY	Possibly
CLIVE	And it's definitely a self-portrait?
HAYLEY	That's the distinctive signature, look. Victor Noble Rainbird. Oh, look. Something else. For Liz. That's unusual
CLIVE	Liz?
HAYLEY	I've no idea
CLIVE	But it will be worth a bit?
HAYLEY	Sure to be
CLIVE	Wait here. I'll have a word with the crustacean (EXITS WITH PAINTING. HAYLEY CONTINUES TO BROWSE. CLIVE EVENTUALLY RETURNS) The old fool didn't have a clue. He wanted £50. I gave him thirty. (THEY LOOK AT PAINTING, SHE ESPECIALLY) Did you hear what I said Hayley? I got the old coot down to thirty quid. We've made a killing. Let's go! (EXIT CLIVE. HAZEL REMAINS WITH PAINTING AND OBSERVES FOLLOWING SCENE).

THE PAST

	(WE ARE IN 1905, A NORTH SHIELDS OFFICE. ENTER FUST. RAINBIRD IS PAINTING AT ONE SIDE)
FUST	Rainbird? Rainbird? Where is that young scamp? (SEES AUDIENCE) Ah. Septimus Fust, chief clerk at the North Shields accounting firm of Campbell & Patterson, and, though I say it myself, a rather accomplished chief clerk at that! Now then, Rainbird! Rainbird! (ENTER JONES, YOUNG EMPLOYEE) Where is he, Jones? Where is Rainbird?
JONES	Not here Mr. Fust
FUST	Yes, yes, I can see that, Jones. So where is he?
JONES	Painting, Mr. Fust

FUST	Painting ?
JONES	Painting pictures
FUST	Painting pictures?
JONES	Well, sketching probably
FUST	Sketching?
JONES	He likes painting and sketching does Victor. He does it all the time
FUST	So is he painting or is he sketching?
JONES	I'd say sketching, more like
FUST	In the firm's time? In the year of our Lord 1905? His 20 minute lunch break finished ten minutes ago!
JONES	Sorry, Mr. Fust
FUST	Yes, well sorry doesn't balance the books Jones. Get Rainbird back here. Immediately
JONES	Yes, Mr. Fust
FUST	We don't pay trainee clerks four shillings a week to mess about with painting. Why, he'll be expecting to build castles on Tynemouth Long Sands next!
JONES	Why would he want to do that, Mr. Fust?
FUST	Just get him back here, Jones
JONES	Yes, Mr Fust (GOES OVER TO RAINBIRD) Fusty says you've to stop that now and get back to clerking
FUST	Nearly finished
JONES	He says now
FUST	Just wanted to draw that big boat. It'll be gone soon

JONES	You'll be gone if you get Fusty mad. Come on (LEADS HIM AWAY. ENTER RALPH WALTER LIDDLE)
LIDDLE	How nice! How very nice! Me? I am a fairly well-known personage in these parts, Ralph Walter Liddle, headmaster – yes, we still called it a headmaster in 1905 – at Tynemouth School of Arts and Sciences and a not inconsiderable painter myself. Perhaps I could just – (GOES TO SHOW HIS OWN WORK)
VOICE O/S	Get on with it!
LIDDLE	Very well. I believe this young man Rainbird possesses a special talent. He was, I believe born for a life of painting and all which that involves. The young fellow attends my night classes and I intend to recommend that he be accepted by Armstrong College, Newcastle, a most worthy institution. I shall also recommend that his work be included in the 1905 Artists of the Northern Counties Exhibition at The Laing Gallery in Newcastle upon Tyne, yet another most worthy institution
RBIRD	Thank you Mr. Liddle for recognising a truly original talent – me. You will be remembered
LIDDLE	And my own paintings? Will they be remembered?
RBIRD	Well –
JONES	But what about your clerking, Victor? What about Fusty? (ENTER FUNCTIONARY)
FUNC	Victor Noble Rainbird, you are awarded the Silver Medal for the highest placed student in all arts subjects at Armstrong College. You are also awarded the Kings Prizeman in design with honours, you are awarded a national silver token for figure compositions and your work is to be included in a national government exhibition to tour New Zealand, Canada and Australia......Oh, me? Just a functionary and my brief part in this play is now finished (EXIT)
RBIRD	Did you hear all that Jones? I'm on my way!

JONES	But what about Fusty?
RBIRD	Poor old Fusty!
FUST	To be quite frank about it, the esteemed accountancy firm of Campbell & Patterson (established 1826) are well rid of young Mr Victor Noble Rainbird, who scarce knows the difference between a fixed asset and a – well, and a non-fixed asset!
RBIRD	Thank you Mr. Fust for your valuable insights into double-entry book-keeping, which I shall always treasure. But now you see, the world is spreading itself before me and demanding to be painted! So, I paint! (BEGINS TO PAINT WITH GREAT ENTHUSIASM. VARIOUS PEOPLE PASS BY AND LOOK. THEY ALL SEEM TO APPROVE. ENTER AGAIN FUNCTIONARY)
FUNC	What? Another speech? From me? Oh good! I read the following letter! We are delighted to inform you that your pupil Victor Noble Rainbird is to be offered a place of study at the Royal Academy of Arts in London
RBIRD	The what? Let me see that letter! (TAKES IT)
FUNCT	No need to snatch
RBIRD	The Royal Academy of Arts in London! Me! A lad from North Shields!
FUNC	A town hardly as fashionable as Kensington, I agree. You may be interested to know, you will be the only student from the north of England to be offered a place at the Royal Academy this entire year
RBIRD	I'm not from the north of England, man
FUNC	Really?
RBIRD	I'm from the North East. They'll probably think I stink of fish – and what if I do? A Rainbird in London ? Hey!

(ENTER WILLIAM)

WILL What do you think of this, Victor? (HAS PAINTING)

RBIRD (EXAMINES) This is yours?

WILL Yeah – why not?

RBIRD Just asking

WILL You're not the only brother with painting talent

RBIRD I'm the only brother going to the Royal Academy of Arts

WILL You?

RBIRD Yes, me, Your little brother Victor

WILL The Royal Academy?

RBIRD That's right

WILL The Royal Academy of Arts? In London?

RBIRD Are you jealous?

WILL But I mean – how – and why – and - (VICTOR SHOWS HIM LETTER. WILL READS) You lucky bastard

RBIRD You are jealous

WILL I could go to the Royal Academy

RBIRD You, big brother?

WILL My painting's just as good as yours. Look! (GETS ONE. SHOWS)

RBIRD Poor old William

WILL What do you mean, poor old William?

RBIRD Well, you know -

WILL	Who's to say your paintings are better than mine, eh?
RBIRD	But they are better than yours
WILL	You seem pretty sure of yourself
RBIRD	About painting? Course I'm sure of myself
WILL	Oh yeah? And what makes you so special?
BIRD	Never mind, William –
WILL	Never mind, never mind! Come on, Mr High and Mighty!
RBIRD	Ok. Listen William. I know you like to paint. But painting isn't just dabbling with a few brushes. A week-end distraction, pass an idle hour. You saw me painting so you thought you'd have a crack at it. I mean, how can it be difficult?
WILL	You talk like you're the only one here allowed to paint
RBIRD	I'm the only one here who lives and breathes it. Is that the same for you, is it? No. Maybe you live and breathe for being a - what is it, a marine fitter? No? Then maybe you just live and breathe, eh? Like many people
WILL	You think you're so special. Maybe I just haven't found it yet, what I live and breathe for
RBIRD	Don't wait too long. Will you? (BEAT)
WILL	I don't need your advice, Victor
RBIRD	Fine. I won't give it, then
WILL	You're an elitist snob, do you know that?
RBIRD	I'm just a painter
WILL	A better painter than your brother, eh?
RBIRD	Unfortunately for you, yes.

	Oh - come here, brother (HUGS HIM)
WILL	Do you know something, Victor? Your paintings are better than mine. And you know something else?
RBIRD	Tell me
WILL	Right this moment, I bloody hate you for it (EXITS. RAINBIRD ENTERS THE ROYAL ACADEMY. HE IS ENROLLING. CLERK IS AT A DESK)
CLERK	(LOOKING DOWN LIST) Rainbird........Rainbird..... Rainbird..... Ah. here we are, Victor Noble Rainbird. Date and place of birth?
RBIRD	Dec 12th 1887, 12, West Percy Street, North Shields
CLERK	North Shields?
RBIRD	That's right. North Shields
CLERK	That's two words, I assume?
RBIRD	You assume correctly, Mr Pen Pusher. Pen Pusher – that's two words, I assume?
CLERK	You are now enrolled in the Royal Academy of Art, a noble and much respected institution. Lectures take place every weekday from 9am. Punctuality is essential, bad behaviour is not tolerated, respect for one's superiors is required at all times. Lunch can be had in the refectory
RBIRD	Lunch?
CLERK	Yes, lunch, 1pm
RBIRD	Oh aye. Dinnertime
CLERK	Lunch. Now, you will be sharing a room with Mr Gerald Brockhurst, a student from the south of England
RBIRD	Never heard of him. Or them

CLERK	Oh, I'm sure you soon will. Mr Brockhurst intends to make quite a name for himself as a portrait painter (ENTER BROCKHURST)
BROCK	I shall indeed. And rightly so. I'll take the right hand bed if you don't mind. Mother told me to avoid draughts at all costs. The name's Gerald Brockhurst. You?
RBIRD	Rainbird, Victor Noble Rainbird
BROCK	How very quaint! From?
RBIRD	I'm from North Shields
BROCK	North Shields – enlighten me!
RBIRD	It's a small fishing town, near the mouth of the Tyne, Northumberland
BROCK	Still not really getting it. Somewhere up there?
RBIRD	Let's just say it's a long way from here
BROCK	What strange diction you have
RBIRD	It's Geordie, man
BROCK	Who?
RBIRD	Not who – what. Geordie
BROCK	I see. Geordie
RBIRD	*Wi divvent taak like yee*
BROCK	I beg your pardon
RBIRD	Nothing, So you paint portraits, do you Brockhurst?
BROCK	I certainly do
RBIRD	Oh aye. And where do you do that?

BROCK	My parents got me a studio in the centre of London. Very convenient
RBIRD	Oh aye. And you paint inside this studio do you?
BROCK	Of course, I want to paint society people, famous people, the kind of people the public like to see
RBIRD	Painting famous people in a studio? And will they pay you, these famous people?
BROCK	I expect them to pay handsomely. You should try it, Rainbird
RBIRD	I paint real life. Real life's not lived in a studio. It's lived out there
BROCK	Yes, well, in my experience, people get quite enough of real life 'out there' as you put it. A miserable business. They need an escape
RBIRD	You can't escape it. And you shouldn't want to. I want to see life and paint it. All of it
BROCK	Really?
RBIRD	You see, Brockhurst, lots of people look at life but they don't actually see it
BROCK	Are all you Northern chappies as argumentative as this?
RBIRD	Aye. And we eat our own children. Boiled normally
BROCK	I don't suppose you get many famous or celebrated people in - where is it? – North Shields
RBIRD	Everyone's famous in North Shields. Mind, just in their own pub. And there are about 10,000 of them. Pubs, that is
BROCK	And what about you Rainbird? Will you be famous, even beyond the lounge bar of one pub?
RBIRD	Why not?

BROCK	Hmmm. Fishing town, you say? A smelly place, I'd reckon
RBIRD	Have you ever been on a small fishing boat, Brockhurst?
BROCK	I should think not!
RBIRD	Me uncle took us out last year in a 30ft long boat, small wheelroom, open deck, men gutting fish in a force eight with the sea breaking over them. I kept throwing up
BROCK	A charming prospect
RBIRD	That's life though, eh?
BROCK	My point exactly
RBIRD	Mine too. One day I'll paint those fishermen and those boats
BROCK	I believe you will
RBIRD	Just like I'll paint them wild hills of Northumberland and its castles and its coastline. And the rest of the world. I'll paint it all. But I'll not be painting the rich and the famous, thank you very much
BROCK	How very noble. My advice to you Rainbird is this. Paint your paintings, keep people happy, don't look for problems. Prosper.
RBIRD	Well, thank you for that
BROCK	And just remember that art is a business, like everything else. Then you won't go far wrong
RBIRD	No, art's not a business. I don't like business
BROCK	I know who you should meet, Rainbird
RBIRD	Who?
BROCK	Augustus John
RBIRD	Augustus John? Is he a painter?

BROCK	Oh yes. He's a real character. He's from one of those farflung places like you are. You two would get on well
RBIRD	So why don't I meet him? (ENTER JOHN)
JOHN	No time like the present, boyo. Augustus John at your service. So, call yourself a painter, do you Rainbird?
RBIRD	I don't need to call myself a painter. I am one
JOHN	Let's have a look then (RAINBIRD PRODUCES SOME PAINTINGS TO SHOW JOHN) Not bad, not bad at all. A little unfocussed at times, but yes. I suspect you would be a fan of the pre-Raphaelites?
RBIRD	They're my favourites
JOHN	Mine too. Don't go shouting that off at the Royal Academy, mind They're not so keen on the Brotherhood there. I put it down to Sir Joshua Reynolds, The Academy founder
RBIRD	You mean Sir 'Sloshua'?
JOHN	Ah, you know that nickname! The pompous oaf. I get a little bit tired of the metropolitan mob sometimes. I'm a provincial like you, you could say. From Wales, boyo
RBIRD	I'd like to see some of your work
JOHN	You'd like it very much – that's an order by the way!
RBIRD	I'm not very good at taking orders
JOHN	Better and better! I'm at The Slade. Though I 'm suspicious of all art institutions and establishments. Just let the painters paint, that's what I say. I'd like to blow all the art institutions up
RBIRD	You'd need a big bomb
JOHN	Wouldn't I just? I have an idea, Rainbird. A little jape, if you will, a joke at the expense of that same establishment and the whole damned art industry. Are you game?

RBIRD   What is it?

JOHN   If you do like my paintings – and how could you not? – you have a go at creating an Augustus John painting. I shall create a Victor Noble Rainbird painting. Up for that, are you?

RBIRD   I don't understand

JOHN   See it as an artistic challenge. A gamble. And also a piece of disruptive fun. You paint yours in my style, I paint mine in your style. You sign yours Augustus John, I sign mine Victor Noble Rainbird. We exchange the paintings. And only you and I will know the truth!

RBIRD   So we don't tell anyone at all?

JOHN   No-one! That's part of the fun! And makes it more interesting! Who knows, one of the paintings may earn one of us a tidy sum! It's a gamble! And if we make fools of all those money-grabbing vultures out there who feed off our talent – serves 'em right, eh? Except we'll never tell them – or they might want their money back!

RBIRD   What an incredible idea

JOHN   Come and see my paintings tomorrow. We provincials – stick together eh, Rainbird? Paint on. More soon. That's me done. (EXITS)

BROCK   Didn't I say you'd like him? (EXITS)

PRESENT DAY

           HAYLEY IS ON HER LAPTOP GOOGLING. ENTER CLIVE ON HIS MOBILE)

CLIVE   (TO PHONE) Really? And you're pretty sure of that? Well thank you Arthur, thank you very much. Yes, we must play a few holes soon, of course. (ENDS CALL. NOTICES HAYLEY) Busy?

HAYLEY   Just Googling Rainbird. He really did create a lot of paintings. Extraordinary. Born 1887, died 1936.

	He didn't live that long. (PICKS UP PAINTING AND HOLDS IT UP ON WALL) What do you think?
CLIVE	What?
HAYLEY	The light on that wall would bring out the painting's vibrant colours
CLIVE	Oh yes. That was Arthur Merrington by the way
HAYLEY	What a tragic life Rainbird had
CLIVE	Investment expert. Knows a bit about art too. You remember Arthur?
HAYLEY	Can't say I do
CLIVE	Bad breath. Handicap of twelve
HAYLEY	A friend of yours?
CLIVE	A colleague, shall we say?
HAYLEY	Rainbird's life ended up with poverty, alcoholism and cancer
CLIVE	According to Arthur, your Rainbird could soon be hot property
HAYLEY	The thing was, somehow he carried on painting, regardless. Then he was buried in a pauper's grave for 80 years. 80 years! Look at that face, Clive. That face could haunt you
CLIVE	Yes, It seems to haunt you Hayley. Anyway, he's hot property. You know the kind of thing, newly discovered past genius from far-flung north. Just what those London big boys really go for according to Arthur. *Pitmen Painters* and all that, he says. Arthur's done a bit of research. Apparently no previous record of a self-portrait. You are certain this is genuine?
HAYLEY	I was studying art when we met as students, Clive, remember?
CLIVE	Of course I remember. Hayley the wild child

HAYLEY   You were a bit of a wild child yourself then

CLIVE   Economics students have to grow up. And enter the real world

HAYLEY   Do you never miss those days, Clive?

CLIVE   Sometimes I think you never got over them

HAYLEY   Anyway. I do know what I'm talking about. This is a genuine Rainbird alright. And I absolutely love it. When I look at this painting, I feel – well, I'm not quite sure what I do feel. But it might inspire me to take up the brushes again

CLIVE   Are you that bored?

HAYLEY   Bored? No, that's not the point, I –

CLIVE   Do start painting again then, Hayley. Hobbies are good for people

HAYLEY   Hobbies?

CLIVE   I knew someone mad on collecting cheese labels

HAYLEY   Cheese labels?

CLIVE   Whatever makes people happy. So - if this painting is genuine, it could soon be worth several thousand pounds

HAYLEY   Is that what your investment expert with bad breath says?

CLIVE   Yes. And likely to rise. And I managed to buy it for only thirty quid. How good is that?

HAYLEY   £30 to several thousand? Doesn't seem quite right somehow

CLIVE   Not right or wrong. Just the market. The shop-keeper agreed on £30. Now we set our own selling price

HAYLEY   What do you mean, our own selling price?

CLIVE   Not for a while of course. Hang on for a time, that's Arthur's advice. An accumulating asset. Keep the painting somewhere

	secure, he says
HAYLEY	What does he mean by that?
CLIVE	He says there are special bank vaults for valuable works of art. Air conditioned, controlled light etc. Total security
HAYLEY	Bank vaults? But I thought that –
CLIVE	You thought what?
HAYLEY	I thought you bought the painting for me, Clive
CLIVE	Well – I bought it for us, I suppose, yes. An investment
HAYLEY	I thought it would look brilliant, right there, on that wall. I could be greeted every morning by Victor Noble Rainbird
CLIVE	Of course. Hang it there overnight. We'll sort out the arrangements tomorrow
HAYLEY	But, a bank vault? Locked away? I think -
CLIVE	You think what?
HAYLEY	I think Rainbird should live here. In this house
CLIVE	It's just a painting, Hayley
HAYLEY	And I think Rainbird wants to live here
CLIVE	A painting. It's paint and canvas and wood. I shouldn't think it gives a toss about where it lives
HAYLEY	It belongs here. Rainbird belongs here
CLIVE	You're being ridiculous. Obsessive. I shall arrange to have the painting picked up
HAYLEY	I don't want it picked up. Rainbird belongs here. Or nowhere
CLIVE	Let's change the subject shall we? Have you decided yet on the menu for Saturday night?

HAYLEY   What?

CLIVE   The menu's important. It needs sorting. Think how much depends on this meal with Blenkinsop and his wife. My boss may be a tosser, but it's his decision whether I get that head office job back in London. We're talking about our whole future here Hayley, which I'm trying to make good. I mean, ask yourself, would anyone in their right mind want to hang around in this neck of the woods for more than two years?? (EXITS. HAYLEY STARES AT PAINTING)

HAYLEY   Actually, Victor, I would

THE PAST.

(RAINBIRD IS PAINTING, HE BREAKS OFF TO BE PRESENTED WITH SEVERAL AWARDS BY THE ACADEMY)

RA   To Victor Noble Rainbird, 1912, £10 and a Silver Medal for Composition in Colour

RBIRD   Thank you! (RETURNS TO PAINTING)

RA   To Victor Noble Rainbird, 1913, £15 and a Silver Medal for a set of four drawings of figures from life

RBIRD   Thank you very much! (SAME)

RA   To Victor Noble Rainbird, 1913, the Landseer Scholarship of £40

RBIRD   Well, thank you again (RETURNS TO PAINTING. ENTER BROTHER WILLIAM)

WILL   You were right Victor. Your brother will never make a painter

RBIRD   William! You came to see me!

WILL   The celebrated Victor Noble Rainbird? You showed all these southerners Victor, I have to admit that

RBIRD   You are proud of your little brother?

WILL   Well…….(BEAT) I have become a poet by the way

RBIRD   A poet?

WILL   Poets can best express the tragedy of the human condition, don't you think?

RBIRD   So William lives and breathes poetry now?

WILL   You ridicule me

RBIRD   Not at all. Why not read me a few lines of your poetry?

WILL   As if you would be interested!

RBIRD   You came down here all this way to tell me you are now a poet. So prove it!

WILL   I'm not sure I can, Victor. You make me feel – self-conscious somehow

RBIRD   William. I am a painter. Here are my paintings for the world to see, good or bad. You are a poet, you tell me. The same principle applies. You cannot be a shy artist. I'm sure you have some poems with you

WILL   I may have

RBIRD   Let your little brother read one (WILLIAM HANDS POEMS TO RAINBIRD WHO READS ONE. PAUSES)

WILL   You don't like my poetry. I can tell

RBIRD   I didn't say that. Sometimes you have to think about a poem and -

WILL   Do you know how hard I work at these poems? How dispiriting it is to come down here and have you dismiss them?

RBIRD   I dismissed nothing

WILL	Back in Shields, all the talk is of Victor Noble Rainbird, a shining star at the Royal Academy. Who ever speaks of his brother? Or his poetry? Give me that back (TAKES POEM)
RBIRD	I thought you might leave a few for me to read. Have you published any poetry yet?
WILL	Do not patronise me! I came here with good intent. Fool that I am (ENTER AUGUSTUS JOHN)
JOHN	Victor, I – (SEES WILLIAM). Oh, you are busy?
RBIRD	Augustus, this is my elder brother William. William, this is Augustus John, a fellow painter
JOHN	Well, hello boyo. You must be very proud of your kid brother then. Quite a star down here, he is. You seen all his medals and – (WILLIAM EXITS) Oh – have I said something wrong, Victor?
RBIRD	William cannot find his destiny. He was hoping it might be in writing poetry
JOHN	And is it any good?
RBIRD	It might not be
JOHN	Anyway, does bloody destiny matter?
RBIRD	My destiny is to paint
JOHN	I don't give a toss about destiny. Let it take care of itself. Why not go after your brother? He seemed upset
RBIRD	What do they say? Am I my brother's keeper? He resents me deeply. I cannot change that
JOHN	He should celebrate his brother. His brother will be a truly famous artist, I know it!
RBIRD	I just paint and carry on painting
JOHN	I can't wait to see your Augustus John painting

RBIRD	Likewise, your Victor Noble Rainbird painting
JOHN	I hope my humble effort earns you a lot of money one day. I'm sure it will
RBIRD	Likewise Augustus. It would give me great pleasure to see my imitation of Augustus John snapped up – and for a big lump sum!
JOHN	I'm sure any painting with the signature Victor Noble Rainbird will be highly valued. I believe the demand for your work will be insatiable
RBIRD	Even my work that isn't my work?
JOHN	Even that. I did my very best to imitate you, you talented bastard. I doubt my name will have your selling power. But if it does – well, that's the gamble. Good luck to me! Good luck to you! Let life always be a gamble! (ENTER BROCKHURST)
BROCK	What is to be done?
JOHN	Done? About what, Brockhurst?
BROCK	This war that's coming against Germany
JOHN	Ah that, yes. Well, a good fight - never did anyone any harm, I say!
BROCK	Rainbird? The war?
RBIRD	I could paint the war. Now that would be something. Just imagine it
BROCK	You imagine it
RBIRD	Imagine the colours, the movement, a landscape swarming with soldiers and equipment. Imagine the emotions, the fear, the glory. Imagine capturing in paint those emotions, that fear, that glory
BROCK	Good luck then. Shoot a German for me

RBIRD	You can't paint a war in a studio, Brockhurst
BROCK	And you can't get shot up the arse in a studio, either
RBIRD	So you'll stay here?
BROCK	What, and risk getting conscripted?
JOHN	There are no plans for conscription
BROCK	Not yet. I'm taking no chances. I shall use my Royal Academy travelling scholarship to move to Ireland. They can't get me there
RBIRD	To paint the rich and famous of Ireland?
BROCK	There's no money in painting the poor
RBIRD	The poor are always with us
BROCK	Always with you maybe. But then you are from North Shields. I'll send you both a postcard (EXIT BROCK)
JOHN	Well, I quite fancy a damned good scrap. Makes a change from a paint palette. Bring it on, I say! Goodbye for now Rainbird (EXITS)
BIRD	My life is changing utterly. What else could happen? (ENTER LIZ)
LIZ	I could happen. Elizabeth Kirkley. I was walking in the city one day when I came across this strange young man with an easle. He was painting York Minster. There was just something about this young man, well – there was just something about him, So I said, why don't you marry me Victor Noble Rainbird?
RAIN	Marry you Liz? Perhaps I just might. But with this war coming? It's hardly the best time
LIZ	There never is a best time, Victor. For anything. There's just time. You love someone, you marry them. Simple

RBIRD	Sometimes I wonder if I am married to my paintings
LIZ	Then commit bigamy. I don't mind
RBIRD	I do love you Liz. You know that? Somehow, you cause everything to make sense
LIZ	Anyway, Victor, if you do go to this war, I want it to be as my husband
RBIRD	But why especially?
LIZ	That way, I shall feel you're - well - you're protected somehow
RBIRD	I am protected. I have a Guardian Angel. She is my creative muse for my painting here on my shoulder, see?
LIZ	Can your muse protect you as much as my love can?
RBIRD	You should ask her. Anyway, isn't it the man who's supposed to ask the woman to marry him?
LIZ	What do those things matter?
RBIRD	You're a remarkable woman, Liz. And perhaps marriage would be good for me. And for my painting. But tell me, how do I paint marriage?
LIZ	You don't have to paint everything, Victor
RBIRD	I do, though
LIZ	Some things are beyond painting
RBIRD	What things? I don't know any. I have an idea, you tell me what to paint and I shall paint it. I shall paint it for you
LIZ	For me?
RBIRD	Yes, exclusively for you. Choose any subject you wish. I shall paint it and present it to you and sign it to you

LIZ   I don't know what to say, what to choose

RBIRD   I could paint you

LIZ   Me?

RBIRD   Portraits are not my strong point, but for you Liz -

LIZ   I don't want you to paint me. (BEAT) I want you to paint yourself

RBIRD   Myself?

LIZ   I want a self-portrait of Victor Noble Rainbird

RBIRD   But I've never done a self-portrait and –

LIZ   And you will never do another. This one will be special, unique

RBIRD   Liz, I'm not sure a self-portrait is really my thing, I -

LIZ   Am I your thing, Victor Noble Rainbird?

RBIRD   You are very much my thing

LIZ   Then you'll paint it. And you'll paint it well. I know I can't have all of you, Victor. Your painting will never allow that. But a self portrait means I always have some of you.
A present I will value for life

RBIRD   I've never even considered taking on such a task

LIZ   Consider it now. (BEAT) You hesitate

RBIRD   I don't know if I can do it

LIZ   If you love me, you can do it. (BEAT) The man who says he must paint everything but cannot paint himself for the woman he loves!

RBIRD   You are mocking me

LIZ	If you don't do this, Victor, you are mocking both of us
RBIRD	Then I shall do it. I shall paint this one self-portrait. I shall paint it for Liz Kirkley, my beloved! But you must sit with me while I paint it
LIZ	I will sit with you every moment you paint. Make this painting as unique as we are unique
RBIRD	There will only ever be one Rainbird self-portrait
LIZ	Only ever one
RBIRD	Yes. And you must never sell this painting, Liz
LIZ	We could always sell it if we were skint! Keep the wolf from the door!
RBIRD	No! I mean it. This is not a painting for sale
LIZ	You do mean it Victor, don't you?
RBIRD	I shall not paint it otherwise
LIZ	Alright Victor. I shall not sell it
RBIRD	No-one must ever sell it

THE PRESENT

(HAYLEY IS PAINTING. CLIVE IS CONFRONTING HER)

CLIVE	What do you mean, you sent them away?
HAYLEY	Just what I said
CLIVE	I went to all the trouble of arranging the transport and storage of the painting and you just sent the removal men away?
HAYLEY	Yes, I did

CLIVE	This is unbelievable

HAYLEY	Don't get over excited, Clive

CLIVE	Over excited? Not only is the painting still here, you've hung it on that main wall in full view of the road outside

HAYLEY	It's the best position

CLIVE	A valuable painting, in full public view? You may as well ask all the crooks on Tyneside – of which I am sure there are several thousand – just to come and help themselves!

HAYLEY	How ridiculous. And what would you lose? The £30 you paid for it, no more

CLIVE	I would lose a valuable investment worth several thousand pounds

HAYLEY	You would lose £30

CLIVE	You're obsessed with that painting (BEAT)

HAYLEY	Anyway Clive, think of the benefits

CLIVE	The benefits?

HAYLEY	Tomorrow night. The important meal with Blenkinsop and his wife

CLIVE	What about it?

HAYLEY	You said you wanted to impress him. So impress him, tell him the story of the Rainbird painting

CLIVE	I have no idea what you are talking about, Hayley. Blenkinsop won't have a clue who Rainbird is, or was

HAYLEY	Of course not. So when you tell him you spotted the painting, recognised its value, bought it for a mere £30, to resell for many thousand – well, what boss would not be impressed with that sort of business instinct? London, here you come

CLIVE	Here *we* come…(BEAT) So this is all for my benefit, you're claiming?
HAYLEY	Why not? Clive, I realise the painting's days in this house are numbered, believe me. But leave it there for tomorrow night please. A favour for me
CLIVE	Let me tell you this Hayley, the sooner we get out of this god-forsaken place and back to civilisation in London, the better
HAYLEY	And then what?
CLIVE	Then anything
HAYLEY	A child?
CLIVE	Like I've told you, once my career is sorted, we can think about that
HAYLEY	I need to create
CLIVE	You have your own work
HAYLEY	I need to create
CLIVE	Create all you like (BEAT)
HAYLEY	Do you know what I'm cooking tomorrow. Clive?
CLIVE	Oh, so you have remembered about the meal? I was beginning to wonder
HAYLEY	We start with a lobster bisque, followed by crispy duck wrapped in parcels, served with a plum sauce. A pudding of bananas coated with lemon juice, put back in their skins, then baked and served with fresh cream and maraschino cherries. Finally, a cheese board, seedless grapes and Nicaraguan coffee. And wine of your choice
CLIVE	What's that if not creative? There are times you amaze me, Hayley
HAYLEY	Your wife has many talents

CLIVE	And here's me thinking you weren't bothered about tomorrow's meal
HAYLEY	I've thought about tomorrow's meal a good deal Clive, believe me
CLIVE	I could almost forgive you hanging that painting. What a busy girl you've been. I saw you at your easel as well
HAYLEY	I thought I might just –
CLIVE	Relive your student days? I understand
HAYLEY	I thought I must just paint
CLIVE	You never quite got over them, Hayley, did you?
HAYLEY	Why should I get over them?
CLIVE	Hayley, this Rainbird thing. It's affecting you rather. Some muddled romantic idea about being an artist. Our student days were fun, of course they were, but we're grown up now, we're sensible and making a life. I have a promising career, soon to be more promising. You have your job with the charity, and very worthy too
HAYLEY	I need to paint the wilds of Northumberland. I need to lose myself in the Cheviots. And on that dramatic coastline. Do you know the film director Roman Polanski claimed the light up here was unlike any he'd ever seen aywhere?
CLIVE	Is that the same Roman Polanski of child seduction fame?
HAYLEY	Painting might just put me back in touch, that's all
CLIVE	Anyway I'm thrilled about your menu. We'll leave the painting up there for the week-end, OK? I'll make other arrangements Monday morning. I hope that is satisfactory (EXITS)
HAYLEY	(TO PAINTING) Is that 'satisfactory' Victor? Would you call that satisfactory

THE PAST

    (WE SEE VICTOR CREATING THE PAINTING. LIZ IS SAT WITH HIM)

RBIRD   (STANDS BACK. SHOUTS OFF) Tell them to delay this war for a bit, would you? Not quite finished painting my self-portrait! There! It's done!

LIZ   Is it good Victor?

RBIRD   What do you think? (SHOWS IT)

LIZ   It is brilliant

RBIRD   But then so is the person who it's for

LIZ   I think you'll be the most handsome soldier, ever

RBIRD   As handsome as my self-portrait?

LIZ   You are your self-portrait

RAIN   I am thrilled you like it

LIZ   I'm proud of it. Like I'm proud of you

RBIRD   Now the painting is part of both of us

LIZ   Does this make us both immortal?

RBIRD   Of course!

LIZ   What else can you create between us, Victor?

RBIRD   Create?

LIZ   The greatest creation any human being can give the world

RBIRD   I'm not quite up to painting a Leonardo, Liz

LIZ   I'm talking about a baby

RBIRD	A baby?
LIZ	Our baby. A baby Rainbird
RBIRD	Babies? Babies are serious matters
LIZ	Babies don't think so. They have lots of fun
RBIRD	Me? A father?
LIZ	Why not? Quite a lot of other men have done it. Or maybe all your power to create goes into your paint brush?
RBIRD	I'll show you about my power to create (THEY EMBRACE)
LIZ	Victor I'm pregnant. I think it's a boy. What shall we call him?
RBIRD	Let us call him Victor
LIZ	I prefer Kirkley
RBIRD	How about both?
LIZ	Let's give him lots of names
RBIRD	Ambrose?
LIZ	Charlie?
RBIRD	Percival?
LIZ	Phillip?
RBIRD	Kenneth?
LIZ	Yes, Kenneth
RBIRD	Let us call him Kenneth Victor Kirkley Rainbird
LIZ	Wonderful
RBIRD	He will be the son of an artist

LIZ	And the son of me as well
RBIRD	Of course......... He is the hope for the future. He is tomorrow Time for me to go to war. I've decided I'll sign up as a private in our own regiment, the Northumberland Fusiliers! What do you think of that, Liz?
LIZ	I think you will survive, Victor
RBIRD	Of course. I am immortal. I have my Guardian Angel! (ENTER ARMY OFFICER)
AO	Attention! (COMES TO ATTENTION) Victor Noble Rainbird. You are now enlisted in the 6th Battalion, Northumberland Fusiliers. You will receive your full training, after which you may well be transferred to the Western Front, (which I have to remind several of those ignorant bastards signing up, is actually positioned abroad). I am instructed to inform you Rainbird that the army may wish to avail themselves of your artistic talents to make field observation drawings. This is dangerous work but essential to the war effort. Lives could depend on the accuracy of your creations. You may be called upon to enter No Man's Land to make such drawings. May your King and Country be proud of you!
LIZ	I shall be proud of you Victor, Your son will be proud of you
RBIRD	Goodbye Liz! I love you!

(BUNTING, MUSIC ETC. FAREWELL TO BRITAIN)

END OF FIRST HALF

SECOND HALF

(WE ARE IN FRANCE. VICTOR IS OBSERVING THE SPECTACLE OF THE WAR POSSIBLY FROM A FIRESTEP IN A TRENCH. AS HE SPEAKS HE BECOMES AFFECTED BY THE BOMBING NOISES WHICH SLOWLY REPLACES THE MUSIC. WAR. LIGHT AND SOUND EFFECTS)

RBIRD Look at it. It is so cruel. Yet so beautiful. It is what we create. It is what then destroys us. How magnificent that sight and sound. It is a painting of wild energy. A symphony unrestrained. And how terrible those weapons are. How beautiful their muscularity. It is a power that could conquer the universe! A power that could destroy that same universe. I am terrified. I am intoxicated. (THE NOISES INTENSIFY AND CLEARLY GET TO HIM. EVENTUALLY HE SINKS TO HIS KNEES, HOLDS HIS HANDS TO HIS EARS).
Have you ever lived close to a war? Ever smelt its foul odours? Its burning flesh? Seen its blood and its guts scattered at random? Its pieces of human beings hurled in every direction? Ever heard the eardrum explosions of shells, on and on and on? Ever heard the last panicked screams of men swallowed in the deep mud of shell craters and no help to be had from those who can hear the screams? Ever tasted human death on your lips? Ever known a colleague in the trenches, his head suddenly blown clean off mid-sentence? Or heard the dying moans of those bleeding to death in no man's land? (SIREN OR WHISTLE SOUNDS)

V/O Gas! Gas! Gas! (GAS ARRIVES. SOLDIERS DON MASKS. EVENTUALLY NOTICE RAINBIRD HAS NOT DONE SO BY WHICH TIME THE GAS HAS GOT TO HIM AND HE IS REACTING, THEY PUT A MASK OVER HIS MOUTH AND DRAG HIM OFF, HE LIES THERE WHILE THE GAS CLEARS. EVENTUALLY AN ARMY DOCTOR ENTERS)

A. DOC How are you feeling now?

RBIRD Headaches. And the chest is tight

A. DOC The chest is the mustard gas. Nasty stuff. Still, we give the Hun as good as we get. Hopefully we got you out before too much damage done. The headaches? A slight onset of shell-

	shock possibly. The incessant barrage. Understandable. Again, only minor I would hope. But overall a few days rest in the army hospital is recommended (ENTER MAJOR)
MAJOR	I'm not sure that is possible right now, Doctor
A.DOC	Not possible?
MAJOR	We are planning a vital assault soon on the salient. Delay could be extremely costly. We need detailed drawings of the enemy's fortifications. Rainbird is by far the best draughtsman we have here. We need him to go into No Man's Land and make some vital sketches
A.DOC	I don't think that is advisable at this particular moment
OFF	Not advisable?
A.DOC	This man needs to recuperate under medical supervision
MAJOR	Men's lives could depend on the accuracy of these drawings, doctor. How are you feeling, Rainbird?
RBIRD	I'm – I'm OK
MAJOR	How would you feel about making some drawings?
RBIRD	I can always make drawings
MAJOR	Course you can. Very important drawings, these are. Men's lives could depend on the accuracy of them. You understand?
RBIRD	Yes, - yes
MAJOR	You just got knocked back a bit, that's all. Getting better already, I can tell. (TO DOCTOR). A whiff of gas – nothing serious. And as for the shell-shock – well the British army is not at all sure that that stuff isn't – let's say, over-exaggerated. How about a nice strong cup of tea, Rainbird? (NO REPLY)
A.DOC	In my medical opinion, this soldier's future wellbeing could be jeopardised if he does not receive immediate treatment.

	Medical opinion is that shell shock can have long term adverse effects
MAJOR	Rainbird, draw me that tree trunk! (HANDS OVER PAPER AND PENCIL. RAINBIRD DRAWS QUICKLY. HANDS OVER) Marvellous. Quite marvellous. Would that I had such talent! Well. Doctor?
A.DOC	Art is an innate talent in him. It doesn't mean he is unaffected in other ways
MAJOR	Thank you doctor. That will be all
A.DOC	But I –
MAJOR	I said that would be all. (DISMISSES HIM) You believe in King and Country, don't you Rainbird?
RBIRD	King and Country?
MAJOR	Yes, the very bedrock of our society. What we are fighting this filthy enemy for
RBIRD	Yes, - yes of course sir…….. Sorry sir – it's the headaches. They come on me suddenly
MAJOR	They will pass. Now, we need some close detail on the enemy's fortification out on that salient. You will need to be in No Man's Land, so proceed with caution. You may need to crawl slowly. Look out for uncollected bodies. Get as close as you can, without jeopardising your own safety of course. As detailed as you can possibly make it, hmmm? This is highly important for the entire war effort. You understand?
RBIRD	I understand, sir
MAJOR	Good man. A few more men like you and this war would soon be over
RBIRD	My Guardian Angel sir
MAJOR	Guardian Angel?

RBIRD	Looks after me. When I'm painting or drawing
MAJOR	That's the ticket, Rainbird. Carry on
	(RAINBIRD NOW SETS OFF INTO NO MAN'S LAND. CONTINUING SOUNDTRACK OF EXPLOSIONS WHICH HE DOES REACT TO. AT TIMES HE STOPS TO DRAW. SOME BOMBS COME CLOSE AND HE REACTS. EVENTUALLY WE HEAR THE LONG APPROACHING WHINE OF A WHIZZ BANG DESTINED FOR HIM. THERE IS A LOUD EXPLOSION WHICH THROWS HIM ONTO HIS BACK. OTHERS LIE AROUND HIM. PASSAGE OF TIME AS HE LAYS THERE. EVENTUALLY A SERGEANT AND PRIVATE APPROACH. SOLDIER IS CARRYING A BUCKET OF LIME. POSSIBLY WHITE FLAG)
SOLD	Burying the dead! Burying the dead!
SERG	That last shell was a big bastard and no mistake. Check all of these bodies, private! (PRIVATE BEGINS TO DO SO) Not that anyone could have survived that blast. Poor bastards. These soldiers will never see English soil again. One minute here, families, wives, sweethearts all thinking of them back home. Next minute, boom, gone. And all that lot back home, not knowing, still thinking of their loved ones and their much awaited return, even as the blood is chilling in their veins. Poor deluded buggers. It's a life, isn't it? (SHOUTS) Make sure you check properly! Mind, dead as a dodo, these are, I reckon. It's a filthy stinking cold muddy mass grave for them. Get that lime on them first private. Don't want them ponging the place out, the Lord rest their wretched souls
PRIVATE	(SPRINKLING LIME) Sergeant! Over here!
SERG	What is it, private?
PRIVATE	I could swear I saw this one's hand move
SERG	Bugger off and shite. These are cold stone dead. Blown to smithereens. Bury 'em
PRIVATE	No, the hand did move, look - just there! (SERG LOOKS)

SERG	Streuth. I think you might be right. Just the teeniest of movements! Well spotted, soldier. Do not bury that man and that's an order! This is a blooming miracle. (RAINBIRD SITS UP)
RBIRD	(SLOWLY) Victor Noble Rainbird – artist. (HOLDS UP DRAWINGS). Im – im – immortal (SLUMPS DOWN)
SERG	Get those drawings off him, private. Could be important. Then get him back to the M.O. (RAINBIRD IS CARRIED BACK ON STRETCHER AND LAID OUT. SOUNDS OF THE SHELLS AND BOMBS CONTINUES AS VICTOR LIES, OCCASIONALLY TWITCHING. WE NOW SEE HIM BEING CARRIED TO A RAILWAY STATION THEN TRANSPORTED BACK TO ENGLAND WHERE HE SLOWLY RISES FROM THE STRETCHER. HE IS BACK IN NORTH SHIELDS. ENTER LIZ. THEY EMBRACE)
LIZ	Let me look at you, Victor. You're thinner
RBIRD	And you look the same as you did
LIZ	It's been so long. And now you're here. Safe. Let me hold you again. Just to make sure it's true (DOES SO). You're shaking
RBIRD	That happens sometimes
LIZ	What causes it?
RBIRD	It will pass
LIZ	There's someone else you should see. Our son
RBIRD	He looks innocent. I thought nothing could look innocent again. I thought innocence had died
LIZ	Victor, there are celebrations all over Shields
RBIRD	Celebrations?
LIZ	The end of the war. All our soldiers returning
RBIRD	Not all of them, Liz

LIZ	No, not all of them. You look tired, Victor. Of course you would. You're home. I'll make you a lovely meal. Better than all that army food, I'm sure! But you must rest first. How strange everything must look to you
RBIRD	Yes, it is all very strange. I will rest, yes. Then maybe I'll be fine
LIZ	It's over Victor. Remember that. It's over (BEAT). You are back to your loved ones. And you must have so much to tell us
RBIRD	Nothing, Liz. I have nothing to tell anyone

THE PRESENT

(CLIVE AND HAYLEY MAKING FINAL PREPARATIONS FOR THE VISIT OF BLENKINSOP AND HIS WIFE)

CLIVE	Everything looks alright, wouldn't you say?
HAYLEY	It all looks fine
CLIVE	And the food's under control?
HAYLEY	It's simmering away nicely, Clive
CLIVE	Impressions are important Hayley. Anything Blenkinsop finds here to his distaste, then the whole promotion and our whole future could be sabotaged. You do understand that, don't you? I am looking out for our future
HAYLEY	Yes, I understand it all perfectly
CLIVE	That's why they invite themselves for a meal. To suss out the bigger picture
HAYLEY	And to suss out your wife?
CLIVE	Like I said, the bigger picture
HAYLEY	Rainbird looks good up there

CLIVE	What? Oh, yes. Let me say, I think you were right this time. The painting story might just impress him. I'll give it an outing anyway
HAYLEY	Yes, do that. I think this painting's going to have a big impact on everything
CLIVE	Well, not quite as big as impact as it's had on you
HAYLEY	A very big impact
CLIVE	Yes, well. Hopefully it will help do the job with Blenkinsop and then your Mr. Rainbird can retire gracefully
HAYLEY	To his dark vault?
CLIVE	To his safe storage. Let's not go into all that again. You look wonderful Hayley. Tell me, what do you know about Chingford?
HAYLEY	Chingford?
CLIVE	Been doing a bit of digging around on London property prices. All things considered, Chingford looks the best bet for a sound property investment
HAYLEY	Property investment? Is that the same as a house?
CLIVE	Just starting to be desirable but still relatively cheap. On the Central Line and the overground. Close to the green belt and rural Essex. Well?
HAYLEY	Chingford……..
CLIVE	I've registered online with some London estate agents. Let's see what comes up in the Chingford area, shall we? Are you excited?
HAYLEY	Excited?
CLIVE	Just imagine. Goodbye to this deadwater. Stick around here and your career's up the spout. It's backward looking, stuck in the past, introspective and all most of them care about is

	Saturday afternoon at St. James Park. I've got ambition for us. Why would we stay here?
HAYLEY	It's never been quite right for you, has it, Clive?
CLIVE	That's an understatement. If you want to make your mark – and what's the point of anything if you don't? - then make sure you're far away from places like this. (DOORBELL SOUNDS). That will be them. I'll answer the door. Ready? (LOOKS ROUND, MAYBE ADJUSTS A COUPLE OF THINGS, THEN EXITS. V/O) Donald! And Marian! What a pleasure! Do come in
HAYLEY	(TO PAINTING) He said Chingford, Victor, Chingford. Me and you. In Chingford

THE PAST

(RAINBIRD IS AT HIS EASEL. DISTRESSED. HE IS DRINKING. ENTER LIZ)

LIZ	I thought we might take Kenneth for a walk, Victor
RBIRD	What?
LIZ	Our son. Take him for a walk
RBIRD	I'm trying to concentrate
LIZ	Are you drinking while you paint?
RBIRD	I seem to be
LIZ	You never did that before
RBIRD	I never painted with a shaky hand before. And the drink helps
LIZ	Drink rarely helps anything in my experience
RBIRD	Liz, I need to get back to this painting. You understand?

LIZ	You will get back to it Victor. Give it time. I have great faith in you. Look, come and spend a little time with your son. Time spent with children is never time wasted
RBIRD	I will Liz, I will. Give me an hour. Please
LIZ	He kicked a football yesterday
RBIRD	A football? Ha! What a clever little man! Newcastle United, here we come! (BEAT) I'm sorry Liz. I just need to –
LIZ	Need to what Victor?
RBIRD	I need to find myself again
LIZ	You will find yourself. And I will help you
RBIRD	We have so very little money
LIZ	I earn what I can at teaching. And drink costs money, Victor
RBIRD	I know
LIZ	Money we don't really have
RBIRD	I know that too
LIZ	You have been through a terrible time. You need to recover, that's all. Drink is not recovery
RBIRD	Painting is recovery
LIZ	I shall take Kenneth out on my own then. I love you Victor. Don't become a stranger (EXIT)
	(A SHIELDS BAR. RAINBIRD APPROACHES)
BAR	Well, Mr Rainbird, isn't it?
RBIRD	A pint and a whisky
BAR	No problem at all, Mr. Rainbird. One pint and one whisky coming up. That will be one and tuppence please

RBIRD	One and tuppence?
BAR	That's what I said
RBIRD	I'll pay you later today
BAR	Course you will. Then you can have the pint and the whisky later today as well
RBIRD	I need it now
BAR	I'm sure you do. Not my problem though, is it?
RBIRD	I told you. I'll pay you later. I – I expect to sell a new painting soon
BAR	That's what you told The Hotspur and The Fleece and the Golden Lion and all those other pubs in Shields. They're still waiting for the dosh, all of them. I wonder when that painting will get sold? I suggest you go home
RBIRD	Home?
BAR	To your wife and child. There's nothing for you here, Mr. Rainbird
RBIRD	But I've got to have a drink. Don't you understand?
BAR	Oh aye, I understand perfectly
RBIRD	Then give me the beer and the whisky!
BAR	You've got to have a drink. I've got to make living. The perfect arrangement. Only one thing missing. The cash
RBIR	Just give me that drink!(GRABS HOLD OF BARMAN)
BAR	Right. Get out of here out, right now and don't come back
RBIRD	I'm sorry, I didn't mean that, I -
BAR	Just another Shields drunk. As if we didn't have enough of them round here already

RBIRD	I'm not a drunk
BAR	Course you're not. They say you were a brilliant painter before the war
RBIRD	I am still a brilliant painter
BAR	A special gift, they said you had
RBIRD	Have you seen my paintings?
BAR	Can't say I have
RBIRD	How would you like to have one of my paintings of your own?
BAR	What for?
RBIRD	It could be worth a lot of money one day
BAR	I don't have any money to spend on the likes of paintings, I'm afraid. Times are hard
RBIRD	I will do you a painting, or maybe a sketch. In return for some drink
BAR	Bit of a bloody cheek. Alright, as a favour. I could always hang it on that wall. It would cover that crack. Save me painting it over. You can have that one pint of beer and one whisky. How does that sound?
RBIRD	One pint of beer and a whisky? For a painting?
BAR	Take it or leave it, Mr.Rainbird
RBIRD	And I get the drink first?
BAR	One drink first, one after. OK? (PRODUCES PIECE OF CARD) Do it on this. Got some painting stuff with you, have you?
RBIRD	I have some charcoal here, I can do a sketch with that
BAR	That's fine. See that trawler in the gut? Could you sketch that?

RBIRD	I can sketch anything
BAR	The trawler would do for now, thanks. It belongs to Alan Morse, a good friend of mine
RBIRD	I need one of those drinks first!
BAR	Fair enough. One drink before. The beer or the whisky?
RIRD	Either!
BAR	There you go then. One very fine whisky (HE DOWNS IT QUICKLY)
RBIRD	And the other one?
BAR	All in good time. Off you go (RAINBIRD BEGINS TO SKETCH. BARMAN LOOKS AT IT). That's coming on very nice. Very nice indeed. You've got a real talent, you have. You could get a nice little number going (LATER GOES HOME TO LIZ)
LIZ	Where have you been, Victor? Or need I ask?
RBIRD	I've been working
LIZ	It doesn't smell like you've been working
RBIRD	I sold some of my art. And more to come
LIZ	Really? You have the money? Oh I see. That was the payment
RBIRD	At least somebody wanted to buy my art
LIZ	Stop feeling sorry for yourself
RBIRD	What?
LIZ	For God's sake do you think you are the only person who matters in this world?
RBIRD	What?

LIZ	I am trying to help you Victor. I love you. Your son loves you. I am doing everything I can to keep this marriage afloat. And you – you are sinking us
RBIRD	Liz, I –
LIZ	No, stay away from me! You frighten me when you are like this. And you frighten Kenneth. Look at us. Just look at us. And you, painting for alcohol. Is that all that your art is worth now? I don't know how much I can take Victor (TURNS AWAY. DR STEPHEN FARRINGTON APPEARS. COMES TO HER. HALF EMBRACES HER BUT SHE PUSHES HIM AWAY)
RBIRD	My art must make us some money
	(RAINBIRD ADDRESSES HIS NEW PAINTING EVENING CLASS. THE SPEECH IS OCCASIONALLY INTERRUPTED BY HIS COUGHING)
RBIRD	I am Victor Noble Rainbird, artist. Welcome to this, the first of my North Shields painting workshops. To paint is to be alive, to interpret the world, to redefine it on your own terms. To make a universe with a brush and paint and paper. And your own imagination. And what you create will be unique, I can guarantee it. Will it be any good? Who knows? Others will decide. Do not let go of whatever talent you have, do not let life, or people squeeze it out of you. Be true to your talent and it will reward you. Make life your inspiration, not your yoke. I am here as your tutor to help and guide you, but no help or guidance is any use without your own innate talent, whatever that talent may be. And talent is something which cannot be faked. It will not suffer pretence or the counterfeit. If you have creative talent – and some of you may discover you do not - cherish and protect it above all things and it will not let you down.(COMES TO THE SIDE TO COLLEGE MANAGER)
MGR	Very good, Mr. Rainbird, very inspiring (HANDS OVER MONEY)
RBIRD	Is that all I get?

MGR	Not much money around these days for art, I'm afraid. We do what we can here at college. Didn't you once know the painter Augustus John by the way?
RBIRD	In our student days, yes
MGR	Doing very well now. I see he's got a big exhibition on in London
RBIRD	Really?
MGR	A piece here in Artists Monthly. Some lovely paintings (RBIRD READS PIECE)
RBIRD	That painting
MGR	What about it?
RBIRD	That painting there. You see it?
MGR	Well, yes,. I see it but –
RBIRD	I must go. Somehow I must get myself to London
MGR	I don't understand, I –
RBIRD	Even if I have to walk. I must get to that exhibition (HE TRAVELS TO LONDON)
	(A LONDON GALLERY. GALLERY MANAGER. ENTER RAINBIRD)
RBIRD	That painting. How much is it worth?
MGR	That one? I think you'll find that one's sold
RBIRD	Sold? How much?
MGR	Let me see. Ah yes, £3,000. Considered one of Augustus John's most interesting works
RBIRD	I painted it

MGR   What?

RBIRD   That painting. It's not by Augustus John. It's by me!

MGR   By you? Ah. Can you see the signature there? It reads, Augustus John

RBIRD   I painted the signature too

MGR   I see. And you are exactly?

RBIRD   Victor Noble Rainbird, North Shields painter

MGR   And you claim to have painted this piece of work?

RBIRD   Years ago in my Royal Academy days. John and I challenged one other to do a painting, each in the style of the other. This is the painting I did in his style! That money rightly belongs to me!

MGR   Ah, the money. Yes, I see now.....

RBIRD   It belongs to me!

MGR   I understand. Where did you say you live, Mr.- erm - Rainbird, is it?

RBIRD   Victor Noble Rainbird

MGR   Extraordinary name

RBIRD   I live in North Shields

MGR   North Shields?

RBIRD   Yes. Tyneside. The North East

MGR   Ah, yes. Up there

RBIRD   I read this painting was to be in his exhibition. I had to come

MGR   Somewhat down on your luck by all appearances?

RBIRD	Ask John himself. He'll tell you. The painting's mine
MGR	Mr. John has already signed the necessary paperwork confirming all the exhibits on show are his own work. Standard procedure
RBIRD	Ask him! He must have forgotten!
MGR	I'm not sure Mr. John is available to see anyone right now, I – (ENTER JOHN)
JOHN	That's alright, Mellors. I'll handle this (TAKES RAINBIRD TO ONE SIDE) Victor Rainbird? Is it you?
RBIRD	Of course it's me
JOHN	I didn't recog– I mean, well, how nice is this! How are you, Victor?
RBIRD	I am not famous. Unike you
JOHN	Fame? What does that mean?
RBIRD	A lot, when you don't have it
JOHN	Good to see you Victor! You survived the war, then?
RBIRD	In a fashion. You clearly did
JOHN	You wouldn't believe this. I was the only British soldier to get sent home from the Western front for fighting!
RBIRD	Really?
JOHN	Really. A few set-tos with officers you see! Bloody pricks, the lot of them. Well, how nice of you to come to my exhibition, Victor
RBIRD	Augustus, that painting, the one of yours that I did
JOHN	I know, sold for £3,000. It's a hoot isn't it, boyo? What about my Rainbird painting? How did that go?

RBIRD	I still have it
JOHN	Ah - well. Time yet. I'm sure it will bring you some cash soon
RBIRD	Augustus – I just thought you might –
JOHN	What?
RBIRD	Give me some of the £3,000 (BEAT) Things have not been so good, you see and it was painted by me after all and -
JOHN	Victor, this was our deal, remember? It was a gamble, for both of us. Now when you sell my Victor Noble Rainbird painting for a tidy sum, as you will, I'm sure, I shall be the first to congratulate you –
RBIRD	But people aren't buying Rainbird paintings and –
JOHN	A gamble, Victor. We live life, we gamble it. That's how it is. With your talents, I'm sure you'll be back on your feet again soon and when you are, you'll regret coming here and asking me this. Believe me
RBIRD	I wouldn't have come unless I had to –
JOHN	(BEAT) Look, boyo, I hate to see a fellow painter down on his luck. Here's £20 as a goodwill gesture. At least it will get you back to – where is it? – North Shields. But do me a favour, eh? Don't spend it on drink. You've a real talent, always remember that
RBIRD	No-one else seems to remember that
JOHN	They will. They will, believe me. Look, I have to go now. I've got an interview with a so-called leading art critic in ten minutes. He knows sod all about art, I tell you, boyo! Which one of them does? Goodbye Victor. Today I am lucky. Tomorrow Victor Rainbird will be lucky. That's the way of it (EXITS)
	(IN COURT. RAINBIRD AND A MAGISTRATE)
MAG	Victor Noble Rainbird, you are accused of being drunk

	and disorderly in North Shields police station last night. According to PC Weatherill, four men brought you in at 11pm by which time you were helplessly drunk. How do you plead?
RBIRD	Victor Noble Rainbird does not plead
MAG	I take that as a plea of guilty. Your solicitor claims your war history of shell-shock and gas poisoning, has had a negative affect on your fortunes. What is your livelihood?
RBIRD	I am a painter
MAG	A house painter?
RBIRD	An artist
MAG	What do you paint?
RBIRD	I paint the world
MAG	The world?
RBIRD	The terrible, cruel, unforgiving world, which I love
MAG	And you earn good remuneration in this employment?
RBIRD	I earn next to nothing
MAG	As this is your first appearance before this court – and I sincerely hope the last – the fine is five shillings. Stand him down
	(VICTOR PAINTING. ENTER LIZ)
LIZ	You are not well at all, Victor. And now you are coughing
RBIRD	I shall get better. Painting will make me better
LIZ	I hate to see you like this. You have never been the same, all those years since the war. Please do not cut your family out
RBIRB	What?

LIZ		Your wife and your son. We are here for you
RBIRD		My wife and my son!?
LIZ		Yes. Here for you
RBIRD		Perhaps it is my wife and my son that has brought me to this!
LIZ		What?
RBIRD		I once told you I was married to my paintings
LIZ		You are blaming us?
RBIRD		Why do people now not buy my paintings? As they once did before all – this happened
LIZ		Before all this happened? I tell you what happened Victor. The war happened. The war left you like a husk. The shell shock. The gas, which probably explains the coughing And if you are ever to get better, you need our deep and caring love and support
RBIRD		I hate them all Liz. The politicians, the generals, the statesmen who sent us there. I hate them. I need my Guardian Angel. Where is she?
LIZ		Your Guardian Angel is not enough. Can't you see?
RBIRD		See?
LIZ		You, the painter, who sees everything. Can you not see yourself? And your life? It is falling apart. And it is breaking my heart. And your son's heart
RBIRD		I – I shall be well again. I need only to paint better
LIZ		No, you won't be well again. Not unless you see. The war has taken a terrible toll on you Victor. It is not your wife and son has done that. Please recognise this. Come back to us. Let us help you. As a family
RBIRD		I am a painter. Or I am nothing

LIZ	You are a human being. And in great pain. Physical and mental pain. I am here, Your son is here. Look at this (SHOWS THE PAINTING). Remember when you painted this? Remember the passion, the energy? (HE LOOKS AT IT). You were the full man. The painter and the human being. And as the full man, you were able to give yourself to me. Not every tiny bit of you. I know that. But enough. Look at Kenneth (ENTER KENNETH). Your blood. My blood. This is our painting. This is our son. This is all part of our life
RBIRD	Am I now to be a failed painter, Liz? How can I live with that?
LIZ	Your work is still exhibited. It's in The Laing, it's in Liverpool Walker Gallery, in the Royal Academy
RBIRD	Mainly old work, not my new work. My main buyers now are the publicans of North Shields. I paint for alcohol. And for bread
LIZ	We can survive. I have my nurse's income, small though it is. But you must have faith in me and in Kenneth. Without that it is impossible. You need us. And we need you
RBIRD	Need me? Who on earth would need me right now? Do my paintings even need me?
LIZ	Please Victor, please, do not drive myself and Kenneth away (THEY EXIT. RAINBIRD SWIGS FROM A BOTTLE. LIZ STANDS SIDE OF THE STAGE. ENTER DOCTOR STEPHEN FARRINGTON)
STEPHEN	How long, Liz?
LIZ	I can't answer that, Stephen
STEPHEN	I offer myself to you. Offer you a good life, you and your son. A secure life as a doctor's wife. And an end to this, this - this miserable penury
LIZ	I know how much you offer. And I thank you for your generosity
STEPHEN	So why the hesitation? He doesn't love you. He loves nothing

LIZ	He tries. But he is unwell. And he cannot see the reality. Don't you understand? The painter cannot see. And now he has problems with his throat
STEPHEN	I can see. I am a patient man. I love you. I ache to be with you. But patience can wear thin. For both you and your son I offer security, devotion, a good and comfortable future
LIZ	I am truly grateful Stephen, understand that. You are a good man, I know that, but before I can do anything, I have to settle things with Victor. I have to know
STEPHEN	Settle things then
LIZ	I cannot just throw love away. Not that easily
STEPHEN	That love, as you call it, is destroying you
LIZ	Perhaps
STEPHEN	I have to go. My surgery awaits. I love you Liz. You know that. It's a proper love
LIZ	I do know that. Goodbye Stephen (THEY EMBRACE. EXIT SEPARATELY)
RBIRD	Where is my protection? Where is my Guardian Angel? I will paint her! (HE NOW PAINTS THE ONLY WAR PAINTING HE PRODUCED AFTER THE CONFLICT WAS OVER, TITLED ALL QUIET ON THE WESTERN FRONT WHICH INCLUDES THE ANGEL OF MONS HOVERING ABOVE A DEAD SOLDIER OF HIS OWN BATTALION WITH A STRIKING RESEMBLANCE TO HIMSELF AND WITH HIS OWN SERVICE NUMBER ON HIS GAS MASK CASE. HE IS STILL PAINTING AND DRINKING WHEN LIZ APPROACHES HIM. HE IS CONFLICTED BUT EVENTUALLY CHOOSES THE PAINTING. THEY LEAVE. HE FALLS INTO A DRUNKEN SLEEP. HE IS STARTLED AWAKE. THE FIGURES THAT NOW APPEAR BEFORE HIM ARE IN HIS MIND. ENTER WILLIAM)

WILLIAM	I found it Victor. I found what I live and breathe for. I am a full time official of the Labour Party which I helped found and which makes me proud beyond measure. I am working for something I truly believe in. To make this a fair country, not one stuffed full of privilege, inequality and terrible injustice where a tiny percentage of the population own a vast percentage of the wealth and land passed down from one generation to the next and seemingly never changing. I intend to help change that for good. Wish me luck brother. I have found my calling. Like you (EXIT. ENTER AUGUSTUS JOHN)
JOHN	Well, boyo, your success, your tours, your exhibitions cannot now be long delayed, surely? A painter of your talent. Did my Rainbird painting ever get sold? Me? I cannot complain. People seem to like my work. Especially my portraits. They sell for very healthy sums. Strange, isn't it? (EXIT. ENTER BROCKHURST)
BROCK	Rainbird! It's Brockhurst. I thought you'd like to know how I'm getting on. Always more rich and famous people wanting their portraits done, it seems. Not that I complain! Did you know I recently painted the famous singer Marlene Dietrich? All good for business, eh?. I never got up there to visit – what was it called again that funny little place? – North Shields. Ah well. (EXIT. ENTER LIZ)
LIZ	You'll be pleased to know Victor that Stephen and I married and are content now and that Kenneth wants for nothing. I'm sure you'll understand when I tell you that Stephen, quite reasonably, found it very difficult to have your self-portrait in the house. I understand. So against my better judgement possibly, we have sold the painting. And that's an end to it. (EXIT BOTH. RAINBIRD MOVES AWAY)
	(ENTER COUNCIL OFFICER)
CO	Victor Noble Rainbird?
RBIRD	Yes. Who are you? If it's for payment of debts, you may as well stand there and whistle a tune
CO	I represent Alderman Armstrong, the Mayor of Tynemouth

RBIRD	What does the Mayor of Tynemouth want with me? He's one of the few people I don't owe money to!
CO	The Mayor wishes to commission you to create a portrait of Earl Haig
RBIRD	Say that again
CO	The Mayor wishes to commission you to create a portrait of Earl Haig
RBIRD	The Mayor of Tynemouth wants me to paint Haig? Me?
CO	You seem surprised
RBIRD	Haig? The man who sent hundreds and thousands of our soldiers to their death in the war?
CO	The supreme commander of the British forces, yes. A controversial figure, agreed. But to many, a national hero
RBIRD	I had no idea the Mayor had even heard of me
CO	Apparently, because of your valuable and accurate field observation drawings, you are spoken of highly as an artist by the War Office
RBIRD	But who's the portrait for?
CO	The painting is to be a present from the council to the Tynemouth British Legion. The Aldermen would like the portrait to show General Haig standing at the salute
RBIRD	Haig should have burnt in hell. Along with the rest of them
CO	I am to inform Alderman Armstrong if you wish to take on this commission (BEAT). The payment is 50 guineas
RBIRD	50 guineas?
CO	A not inconsiderable sum. The council particularly wanted the portrait to be done by a leading local artist, not an outsider. You were the obvious choice

RBIRD	Leading local artist? I don't think so
CO	What am I to tell the Alderman?
RBIRD	Tell him, tell him Rainbird is now only good, painting for pints of beer. (PAUSE) Well?
CO	If I may be so bold, Mr. Rainbird -
RBIRD	Bold? What do you mean?
CO	What I mean is this. My own humble opinion, for what it is worth is that this war which we speak of has brought you much misfortune over the years. It deserves to bring you some small benefit
RBIRD	Carry on
CO	Your own financial circumstances are obviously not all they could be. Painting for pints of beer, as you put it, to my mind humiliates you both as a person and as an artist
RBIRD	You don't think painting Haig would humiliate me?
CO	No, I do not. History will make up its own mind on Earl Haig. Whatever that decision, I think history would thank Victor Rainbird for creating his interpretation of the man. And for you, fifty guineas would clearly bring at least some temporary financial relief. I believe your own talents as an artist have been sadly neglected in recent years. Many reasons. Ironically, the War Office believes in those same talents. To turn down this commission would to my mind be an act of self-damaging folly
RBIRD	You like my work then?
CO	You have painted your own Tyneside powerfully. But also biblical paintings, mythological paintings, paintings from that same war. You have painted the towns of Europe. You have created stained glass windows in this country and abroad. You have nurtured the young artists of our town with your workshops. Now you risk your own obscurity

RBIRD	My body is tired. My brain is tired. My life, I think is over.
CO	Not quite yet, Mr.Rainbird
RBIRD	You know enough about me to know I rarely do portraits. Only once. I painted a self-portrait for the woman I loved and who loved me. It was a painting beyond commerce or money. Yet now it has been sold. Sold!
CO	For your own sake, please accept this commission, Mr. Rainbird. Do not damage yourself further. For the sake of your art, paint this painting
RBIRD	(BEAT) I accept the commission. Please thank the Mayor. And thank you for your words. Who are you exactly?
CO	My identity does not matter Good day, Mr.Rainbird (EXITS)
RBIRD	Haig? Bloody, bloody Haig? (ALLOWS HIMSELF A RARE LAUGH. HE SETS TO CREATING THE PAINTING WHICH WE EVENTUALLY SEE PROJECTED ONTO THE SCREEN) How laughably ironic

THE PRESENT

CLIVE	We're in. I know it! That London job will be mine! Blenkinsop's impressed. He loved your cooking too. Loved the story of the painting. Thought you were the perfect hostess. Excellent! Chingford here we come. I'll see them out (EXITS. ENTER RAINBIRD. HE TAKES UP A KITCHEN KNIFE AND HANDS IT TO HAYLEY. THEY LOOK AT THE PAINTING)
HAYLEY	Not for you, eh Victor? A cold darkness in London? Nor for me (SHE RAISES THE KNIFE THEN SLASHES THE PAINTING MANY TIMES. ENTER CLIVE TO VIEW THE SCENE)

BLACKOUT

MUSIC

>IMAGE COMES UP OF SIMPLE CROSS OF THE PAUPER'S GRAVE IN PRESTON CEMETERY BEARING THE ROUGH WORDS *VICTOR NOBLE RAINBIRD*. THIS DISSOLVES INTO IMAGE OF THE RECENT NEW RAINBIRD HEADSTONE

END OF PLAY

CLOUD NINE THEATRE

was set up in 1998 and in 2018 celebrates its twentieth anniversary. It only produces new work and only by northern writers. It commissions both large and small scale plays and in May 2018 will be performing at The Prague Fringe Festival with a production of *A Parcel for Mr. Smith* which it originally produced for a small tour in the North East in 2015.

Plans for later in 2018 includes a revival of Kitty Fitzgerald's play *Making Plans for Jessica*, and Mary Pickin's *The Battling Ettricks* as part of a special anniversary celebration. The Exchange, North Shields is now the company's natural home.
For more information or to be put on our mailing list, contact us at 0191-2531901
<cloudninetheatre@xlnmail.com>.
See our Website for more details
<www.cloudninetheatre.co.uk>

IRON PRESS

IRON Press is among the country's longest established
independent literary publishers.
The press began operations in 1973 with IRON Magazine
which ran for 83 editions until 1997. Since 1975 we have
also brought out a regular list of individual collections of
poetry, fiction and drama plus various anthologies ranging
from *The Poetry of Perestroika*,
through *Limerick Nation*,
100 Island Poems and *Cold Iron, Ghost Stories
from the 21st Century*.

The press is one of the leading independent publishers
of haiku in the UK.
Since 2013 we have also run a regular IRON Press Festival
round the harbour in our native Cullercoats.
IRON in the Soul, our third festival,
took place in Summer 2017.
Plans are afoot for a 2019 festival.

We are delighted to be a part of Inpress Ltd,
which was set up by Arts Council England to support
independent literary publishers.
Go to our website (www.ironpress.co.uk)
for full details of our titles and activities.